Built for Cold
Arctic Animals

Wolverine
Super Strong

by Joyce Markovics

Consultant: Kris Inman
Assistant Director, Greater Yellowstone Wolverine Program
Wildlife Conservation Society

BEARPORT
PUBLISHING

New York, New York

Credits

Cover and Title Page, © tbkmedia.de/Alamy; TOC, © Anna Yu/iStockphoto; 4, © D. Robert Franz/Rolf Nussbaumer Photography/Alamy; 5, Courtesy of Dr. Audrey Magoun; 6, Courtesy of Dr. Audrey Magoun; 7L, © Peltomaeki/blickwinkel/Alamy; 7R, © imagebroker.net/SuperStock; 9L, © Daniel J. Cox/Natural Exposures; 9R, © Andy Rouse/DRK Photo; 10, © Daniel J. Cox/Natural Exposures; 11, © Igor Shpilenok/Nature Picture Library; 12T, © All Canada Photos/SuperStock; 12B, © Robert Harding Picture Library/SuperStock; 13T, © Wild Wonders of Europe/Widstrand/Nature Picture Library; 13B, © Mark Raycroft/Minden Pictures/Getty Images; 14, © Daniel J. Cox/Natural Exposures; 15L, © James Warwick/Photographer's Choice/Getty Images; 15R, © Rick Dalton-Wildlife/Alamy; 16, © Pierre Vernay/Bios/Peter Arnold/Photolibrary; 17, © tbkmedia.de/Alamy; 18T, © Pierre Vernay/Bios/Peter Arnold/Photolibrary; 18B, © Wild Wonders of Europe/Widstrand/Nature Picture Library; 19, Courtesy of Dr. Audrey Magoun; 20, Courtesy of Dr. Audrey Magoun; 21, Courtesy of Dr. Audrey Magoun; 22T, © Jeff Copeland/The Wolverine Foundation, Inc.; 22B, Courtesy of Dr. Audrey Magoun; 23L, © tbkmedia.de/Alamy; 23R, © Daniel J. Cox/Natural Exposures; 24, © Steven J. Kazlowski/Alamy; 25, © Chris Arend/Alaska Stock LLC/Alamy; 26, © Gerard Lacz/Animals Animals Enterprises; 27, © Daniel J. Cox/Natural Exposures; 28, © Tom & Pat Leeson; 29T, © All Canada Photos/SuperStock; 29B, © Robert Postma/First Light/Getty Images; 31, © Anna Yu/iStockphoto.

Publisher: Kenn Goin
Senior Editor: Lisa Wiseman
Creative Director: Spencer Brinker
Photo Researcher: Picture Perfect Professionals, LLC

Library of Congress Cataloging-in-Publication Data

Markovics, Joyce L.
  Wolverine : super strong / by Joyce Markovics.
    p. cm. — (Built for the cold—arctic animals)
  Includes bibliographical references and index.
  ISBN-13: 978-1-61772-131-1 (library binding)
  ISBN-10: 1-61772-131-X (library binding)
  1. Wolverine—Juvenile literature. I. Title.
  QL737.C25M294 2011
  599.76'6—dc22
                              2010037207

For more information, write to Bearport Publishing Company, Inc., 101 Fifth Avenue, Suite 6R, New York, New York 10003. Printed in the United States of America in North Mankato, Minnesota.

113010
10810CGA

10 9 8 7 6 5 4 3 2 1

Contents

An Arctic Search

It was 2007, and from up in a small airplane **biologist** Audrey Magoun was scanning the snowy Alaskan ground below. She was on the lookout for a wolverine. She had been studying the animals for the past 30 years. Suddenly, she saw a ball of brown fur below. Audrey's excitement grew. Could this be the animal she was looking for?

A wolverine in Alaska

This sighting reminded Audrey of a time earlier in her career when she **tracked** a male wolverine named Roody. Finding Roody had not been easy. The plane Audrey was traveling in had to make several passes over the white, treeless **tundra** where Roody lived. Yet Audrey still couldn't spot him. Finally, though, she saw something below. "I realized it was the brown fur of the wolverine caked with blowing snow," said Audrey. However, Roody was not moving. Audrey feared that the wolverine was dead.

Audrey, shown here, loves studying wolverines because they are so rare and very little is known about them.

Roody was a wolverine that Audrey had previously put a **radio collar** on. His collar gave out a signal that helped Audrey track his movements.

Wolverine Surprise!

Audrey needed to get a closer look. So the pilot landed the plane about 50 feet (15 m) from where Roody was lying. When Audrey hopped out of the plane, she could see Roody's bushy tail poking out of the snow. The front of his body, however, was buried under a snowdrift.

Audrey in the area where she spotted Roody

All of a sudden, Audrey saw Roody twitch. To be sure that Roody was okay, Audrey decided to gently tug his tail. "When my hand was only four inches (10 cm) from his fur," she said, "there was a sudden explosion of snow, fur, and **guttural** rumbling—and there I was face-to-face with Roody!" Seconds later, the surprised wolverine sped away across the tundra.

When Audrey looked inside the hole Roody had been in, she discovered what he'd been doing—eating a frozen ground squirrel. Wolverines sometimes bury food in **caches** during the summer. They do this so that they don't go hungry when food is **scarce** during the long, cold winter.

A ground squirrel

This wolverine is looking for food in the snow.

Home on the Roam

Even though Audrey has spent many years tracking wolverines, she sometimes still has problems finding them. Wolverines are rare, and they live alone most of the time. Also, they make their homes in **remote** places, such as the frozen tundra, in thick forests, or high in the mountains in the **Arctic region**. What else makes wolverines hard to track? "They're on the go all the time," said Audrey.

Wolverines in the Wild

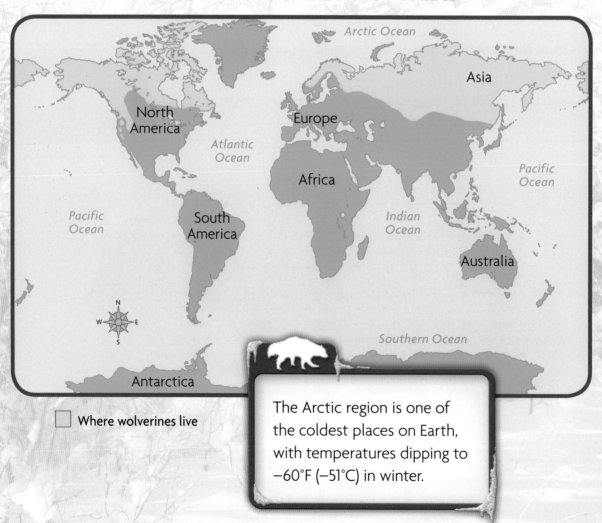

☐ Where wolverines live

The Arctic region is one of the coldest places on Earth, with temperatures dipping to −60°F (−51°C) in winter.

To find enough food, wolverines travel nonstop. As they move, they cover a lot of ground. Wolverines have a huge **territory**, or range. Audrey discovered that female wolverines roam over an area of land that is about 38 square miles (98 sq km). That's close to the size of 18,000 football fields! Males have an even larger range—they roam over an area of land about 115 to 308 square miles (298 to 798 sq km).

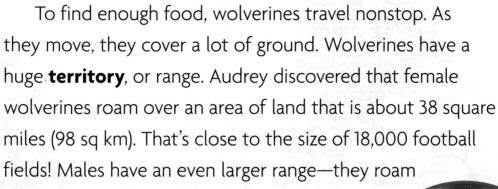

Some wolverines cover 25 miles (40 km) a day—that's about the same distance that a human runs in a marathon.

Wolverines are always on the go. They spend most of their time looking for food.

What's for Dinner?

Since food is scarce in the Arctic, wolverines eat whatever they can find. Sometimes they hunt living animals for food, including ground squirrels, snowshoe hares, **marmots**, birds, and larger animals such as **caribou**.

A wolverine having a meal

Most of the time, however, wolverines eat **carrion**—animals that are already dead. In fact, wolverines are one of the more important **scavengers** in the Arctic. They will even devour dead animals that carry diseases. On top of that, they're determined and fearless when looking for a meal. Biologist Bob Inman knows of two wolverines that competed with black bears for an elk **carcass**, even though the bears were about ten times bigger. "As a result, the wolverines ended up being killed by the bears, but that just shows how **tenacious** they are," said Bob.

This wolverine is feasting on a bear.

Some wolverines will follow wolf **packs** for hours, hoping to gulp down the wolves' leftovers, including elk and caribou meat. This can be risky for wolverines as they are sometimes attacked and killed by the much larger wolves.

What's in a Name?

Despite the name *wolverine*, these animals are not related to wolves. In fact, wolverines are part of the weasel family, which includes ferrets and minks. They're actually the largest members of the weasel family that live on land. According to Audrey, wolverines are about 30 times bigger than their weasel cousins.

Ferrets, such as this black-footed ferret, usually weigh no more than three pounds (1.4 kg).

The wolverine's scientific name is *Gulo gulo*, which means "**glutton**."

Minks such as this one usually weigh between two and four pounds (.9 and 1.8 kg).

Wolverines are very powerful animals. In fact, some scientists consider them to be the strongest of all **mammals** for their size. Females usually weigh between 13 and 26 pounds (6 and 12 kg), and males weigh between 22 and 55 pounds (10 and 25 kg). While these animals are about the same size as a family dog, they appear a lot larger. That's because they are covered with shaggy, thick fur that hides the shape of their bodies.

Wolverines are solidly built and look a lot like short, stocky bears. They are sometimes called "devil bears."

An American black bear

Fabulous Fur

So just how do wolverines survive in the freezing Arctic? They can live in such **extreme** weather because they are **adapted** to life in the cold. For example, their dark, thick, furry coats have two layers of hair to protect them from the fierce cold. The top layer is made up of coarse hair that is up to four inches (10 cm) long. The bottom layer is short and fluffy. Their coats help them stay dry and warm during long Arctic winters.

There's a light brown or creamy band of fur on each side of the wolverine's thick, warm coat. A wolverine also has a mask of black fur around its eyes and on its nose. Some have golden eyebrows.

Wolverines have adapted to the Arctic in other ways, too. Their furry paws are long and wide. They act like snowshoes, keeping the wolverines from sinking into the snow. Their paws allow them to tunnel through deep snow as well. Wolverines also have long claws that enable them to hold on as they scramble up trees and tall rocks to find food or to escape a **predator**, such as a wolf.

Long claws as well as strong muscles help wolverines easily climb trees.

A wolverine can use its claws to dig through nearly four feet (1 m) of snow and ten inches (25 cm) of soil in just minutes!

Mighty Jaws

Besides having warm fur and long claws, wolverines also have powerful jaws, which allow them to eat frozen meat and bones during winter. Just how strong are their jaws? Audrey has captured wolverines in steel cages a few times. More than once, in order to escape, the animals have used their jaws to weaken the steel until it snapped!

This wolverine is using its strong jaws and teeth to feed on this frozen meat.

The jaws of a wolverine are not just for eating and escaping. Wolverines are able to clamp down on and drag very heavy things with their mouths. They are strong enough to drag a mountain goat carcass or the giant leg of a moose, which can be three times their weight, for a few miles.

Wolverines have special upper teeth in the back of their mouths that are angled sideways. They act like knife blades, allowing the wolverine to scrape and slice flesh off bones.

Similar to dogs, wolverines use their jaws and teeth to chew on bones until they are a pile of splinters.

Follow That Smell

Wolverines find much of their food using their keen sense of smell. With their noses, they can locate meat buried deep under the snow as well as follow the trails of other animals to track down food. Wildlife photographer Antti Leinonen knows about the animal's incredible sense of smell firsthand.

This wolverine hopes its nose will lead it to its next meal.

Wolverines sometimes stand up on their back legs to sniff the air to track down food.

In 2000, Antti was looking for wolverines to photograph in a forest in Finland, a country in Europe. However, he was having little luck finding the rare animals. One day, he climbed a tall pine tree and placed a piece of meat near the top, hoping to attract wolverines. Soon, he heard something at the tree's base. When he looked down, he saw a wolverine looking right up at him! The wolverine had used its nose to sniff out the meat.

Scientists sometimes hang meat from a tree in an area where wolverines live. Then in a nearby tree, they set up a camera that detects motion. When a wolverine finds the meat, the camera snaps a photo. This kind of work helps scientists identify and learn more about wolverines.

This female wolverine is trying to reach the moose head that's hanging above her. Audrey Magoun placed the moose head there in order to get the wolverine to climb the tree so that she could take photos.

Communicating by Scent

The wolverine's sense of smell is important in other ways, too. Each wolverine has its very own **scent**, which is recognized by other wolverines. Males and females use their special scent to mark their territory. They do this by **urinating** or rubbing their bellies on the ground. While males fiercely defend their territory against other males, they will allow some females to live in it.

A male wolverine marking his territory

A male wolverine also uses its sense of smell to find a female to **mate** with. Breeding usually takes place from May to August. A male can tell if a female is ready to breed just by sniffing her. After mating, female wolverines give birth about seven to nine months later when it's winter. Giving birth at that time of the year helps keep the small, white **cubs** safe from predators because they can blend into the snowy ground.

A female wolverine may live in the same range as a male, but they do not live together as a family.

Like skunks, wolverines have special glands near their tails that release a stinky fluid when the animals are feeling threatened. As a result, wolverines are sometimes called "skunk bears."

Baby Wolverines

Between February and March, females usually give birth in **dens** that they build themselves out of fallen trees, or in snow caves that they find already built. The caves may have one or two tunnels that can be up to 60 yards (55 m) long. Inside, the females will have two or three cubs.

A wolverine den built at the base of a fallen tree

Cubs are covered with white fur when they are born. However, their fur darkens after a week or so.

A newborn wolverine cub

At birth, the cubs weigh less than one pound (0.5 kg) each—about as much as a loaf of bread. For about the first eight weeks, cubs drink their mother's milk. After nine or ten weeks, they begin eating solid food and start to grow very quickly. The cubs may remain in their mother's home range for as little as six months or for as long as two years.

Wolverine cubs

A mother wolverine with her cub

Many Threats

Once young wolverines reach adulthood, they face many challenges to their survival. There is often little food and deadly diseases in the places where they live. Others may be killed by wolves, bears, or adult male wolverines. In a few places, such as Montana and Alaska, **trappers** catch wolverines for their fur.

In the 1800s, many wolverines were trapped for their warm fur, which was used to line winter coats. Today, trappers such as this one are only able to legally trap wolverines in Montana and Alaska.

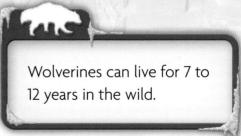

Wolverines can live for 7 to 12 years in the wild.

However, wolverine numbers are most significantly affected by **habitat** loss. "The increasing **human footprint** on the landscape is probably the greatest threat to wolverines," says Audrey. For example, in Alaska and Canada, human activities such as oil drilling, road building, and **logging** drive the animals away. Wolverines that don't have enough space to find food starve to death. They also may not be able to find other wolverines to mate with.

Habitat destruction, which occurs during activities such as the construction of oil pipelines, is driving wolverines away from their homes.

What the Future Holds

"*Gulos* [wolverines] don't need a few secure areas to survive. They need lots of secure areas," says biologist and wolverine lover Douglas Chadwick. To conserve wolverines, Douglas and other experts agree that their Arctic home must be protected. This means limiting development in the places where wolverines could be affected. With help from the government, new laws could be created to save the wolverine's habitat.

A wolverine taking a much needed rest

Wolverines move around a lot, making it very hard to count them. This is the reason that scientists don't know exactly how many wolverines are living in the wild.

More research is also needed to help the wolverine. The more people know about these mysterious and tough creatures, the more that can be done to protect them. For many, wolverines represent a huge part of what makes the Arctic wild and wonderful.

Wolverine Facts

Wolverines are powerfully built scavengers. With shaggy, thick fur for warmth and short legs with wide feet for moving across the snow, wolverines are perfectly adapted for life in the Arctic. Here are some other facts about these amazing animals.

Weight:	females weigh 13 to 26 pounds (6 to 12 kg); males weigh 22 to 55 pounds (10 to 25 kg)
Length:	head and body measure about 26 to 34 inches (66 to 86 cm); tails are usually 7 to 10 inches (18 to 25 cm) in length
Food:	carrion, but wolverines also hunt ground squirrels, snowshoe hares, marmots, birds, and caribou
Life Span:	about 7 to 12 years
Habitat:	Arctic region
Population:	unknown

More Arctic Animals

The Arctic region is one of the harshest habitats on Earth. Only animals that are adapted to extreme cold, such as the wolverine, can survive there. Here are two more.

Caribou

- The caribou is a member of the deer family. Caribou roam the Arctic, feeding on grasses, mosses, and other plants. They use their large, flat hooves to dig for food deep under the snow.
- Both males and females have huge antlers. The caribou's antlers can grow up to five feet long (1.5 m) and weigh as much as 20 pounds (9 kg).
- Caribou are covered with two layers of fur, which protect them from the harsh, icy weather.
- As many as 100,000 caribou travel together in large groups called herds. The herds travel up to 1,600 miles (2,574 km) each year.

Ptarmigan

- A ptarmigan (TAR-mih-jen) is a type of bird that's related to the **grouse**. It's preyed on by wolverines and other Arctic animals.
- Ptarmigans' feet are completely covered with warm feathers. Their feathery feet are a lot like snowshoes, allowing them to easily walk across snow-covered ground.
- During the winter, the ptarmigan's feathers are white, helping it blend in with the snowy environment. In summer, its feathers are mostly brown, helping it blend in with the Arctic's summer colors. This change in color helps ptarmigans avoid enemies all yearlong.

Glossary

adapted (uh-DAP-tid) changed over time to live in a particular environment

Arctic region (ARK-tic REE-juhn) the northernmost area on Earth; it includes the Arctic Ocean, the North Pole, and northern parts of Europe, Asia, and North America; one of the coldest areas in the world

biologist (bye-OL-uh-jist) a scientist who studies plants or animals

caches (KASH-iz) hiding places for supplies of food that are stored for later use

carcass (KAR-kuhss) the dead body of an animal

caribou (KA-ri-boo) large mammals that are part of the deer family

carrion (KA-ree-uhn) dead, rotting animal flesh

cubs (KUHBZ) baby wolverines

dens (DENZ) animals' homes; hidden places where animals sleep or have babies

extreme (ek-STREEM) very great or severe

glutton (GLUHT-uhn) an animal or person who is greedy for food or other things

grouse (GROUSS) a small, round bird

guttural (GUHT-uhr-uhl) low, harsh sounding

habitat (HAB-uh-tat) a place in nature where a plant or animal normally lives

human footprint (HYOO-muhn FUT-print) the impact of humans on the environment

logging (LOG-ing) the cutting down of trees

mammals (MAM-uhlz) animals that are warm-blooded, nurse their young with milk, and have hair or fur on their skin

marmots (MAHR-muhts) bushy-tailed rodents that are part of the squirrel family

mate (MAYT) to come together to produce young

packs (PAKS) groups of animals that live and travel together

predator (PRED-uh-tur) an animal that hunts other animals for food

radio collar (RAY-dee-oh KOL-ur) an electronic device placed around an animal's neck that sends out signals allowing the animal to be tracked

remote (ri-MOHT) far away or difficult to reach

scarce (SKAIRSS) hard to find

scavengers (SKAV-uhn-jurz) animals that feed on the dead bodies of other animals

scent (SENT) an animal's odor or smell

tenacious (tuh-NAY-shuhs) persistent

territory (TER-uh-tor-ee) an area of land that is defended by an animal or a group of animals

tracked (TRAKT) followed someone or something

trappers (TRAP-urz) people who catch wild animals in traps for their fur

tundra (TUHN-druh) a cold, treeless land where the ground is always frozen just below the surface

urinating (YOOR-uh-nate-ing) passing liquid waste from the body

Bibliography

Chadwick, Douglas H. *The Wolverine Way*. Ventura, CA: Patagonia Books (2010).

Alaska Department of Fish & Game:
www.adfg.state.ak.us/pubs/notebook/furbear/wolverin.php

The Wolverine Foundation, Inc.:
www.wolverinefoundation.org

Read More

Markle, Sandra. *Wolverines*. Minneapolis, MN: Lerner Publications (2006).

Somervill, Barbara. *Animal Survivors of the Arctic*. New York: Franklin Watts (2004).

Swanson, Diane. *Welcome to the World of Wolverines*. Vancouver, Canada: Walrus Books (2007).

Learn More Online

To learn more about wolverines, visit
www.bearportpublishing.com/BuiltforCold

Index

About the Author

Joyce Markovics is an editor, writer, and orchid collector. She is grateful for scientists like Audrey Magoun who devote themselves to studying Earth's wildest creatures.